Quilt Notes

This collection of quilts has a quilt for every color of the rainbow. These one-color quilts make selecting fabric so easy that you may decide to make all your quilts of one color. Instead of checking to see if this blue goes with that green or this red, you can look at all the gorgeous fabrics of one color and select as many as you need for that quilt design. One-color quilting also means it is easy to use any color for a quilt. If a quilt is in red and white, it is very easy to change the design to a blue-and-white quilt or a yellow-and-white quilt. All you need to know is the favorite color of the person for whom you are making the quilt or the room in which the quilt will be displayed.

Of course, there are times when you just won't know what color to make a quilt. For occasions like those, or for that special friend who likes a variety, instructions are given for two scrappy quilts that include every color of the rainbow.

Table of Contents

Strawberry Red Album 2

Old-Fashioned Sunshine......7

Thanksgiving......................11

Tree of Life 15

Dream Catcher Delight......21

True Lover's Knot..............26

Four-Patch Diamonds 32

Rainbow Illusions 38

Log Cabin Color Blocks 42

Wilson
91 Utica Ave
Haddon Township, NJ 08108

Strawberry Red Album

BY RUTH SWASEY

Strawberry prints combine with red and white fabrics to make this summery-looking album quilt.

Project Specifications
Skill Level: Intermediate
Quilt Size: 84" x 92½"
Block Size: 12" x 12"
Number of Blocks: 42

Fabric & Batting
- ¾ yard each strawberry prints 1, 2 and 3
- 3¼ yards white solid
- 3 yards red print 1 for blocks
- 1 yard red print 2 for border
- Backing 88" x 97"
- Batting 88" x 97"

Supplies & Tools
- Neutral color all-purpose thread
- Basic sewing supplies and tools

Project Notes
If you prefer traditional piecing, patterns are given for template shapes. Cut as directed on each piece to make one block.

Red is listed on templates without differentiating between red print and strawberry prints.

Instructions
1. Cut six strips white solid and 12 strips red print

Album
12" x 12" Block

1 2⅝" by fabric width. Sew a white strip between two red strips; press seams toward red. Repeat for six strip sets; cut into 2⅝" segments to make 84 B-B-B units as shown in Figure 1.

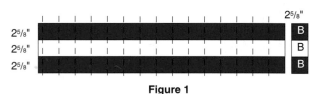

Figure 1
Cut into 2⅝" segments to make B-B-B units.

2. Cut seven strips white solid 2⅝" by fabric width. Cut into 6⅞" segments for D; you will need 42 white solid D segments.

3. Cut 20 strips 2⅝" by fabric width red print 1. Cut into 6⅞" segments for D; you will need 120 red print 1 D segments.

4. Cut eight strips 2⅝" by fabric width red print 1.

HOUSE OF WHITE BIRCHES, BERNE, INDIANA 46711   WWW.WHITEBIRCHES.COM

Cut into 2⅝" square segments for B; you will need 120 red print 1 B squares.

5. Cut two strips each 2⅝" by fabric width strawberry prints 1 and 2. Cut into 2⅝" square segments for B; you will need 24 each strawberry prints 1 and 2 B squares.

6. Cut four strips each 2⅝" by fabric width strawberry prints 1 and 2; cut into 6⅞" segments for D. You will need 24 each strawberry prints 1 and 2 D segments.

7. Cut four strips white solid 3⅜" by fabric width. Cut into 3⅜" square segments; you will need 42 squares. Cut each square on both diagonals to make A triangles. You will need 168 white solid A triangles.

8. Cut 18 strips white solid 3" by fabric width. Cut into 3" square segments; you will need 252 squares. Cut each square on one diagonal to make C triangles. You will need 504 white solid C triangles.

9. To piece one block, sew C to opposite sides of a B square as shown in Figure 2; add A. Repeat for four A-B-C units.

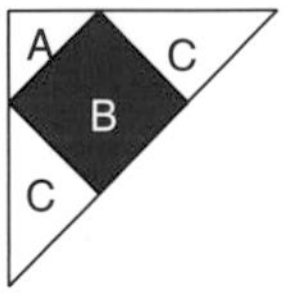

Figure 2
Sew C pieces to B; add A.

Figure 3
Sew C to D.

10. Sew C to short sides of D as shown in Figure 3; repeat for two C-D units.

11. Sew a B-B-B unit to opposite long sides of D as shown in Figure 4.

Figure 4
Sew 2 B-B-B units to D.

12. Arrange pieced units with two D's as shown in Figure 5; join to complete one block. Press; repeat for 18 red-and-white blocks and 12 strawberry print 1 and 12 strawberry print 2 blocks as shown in Figure 6.

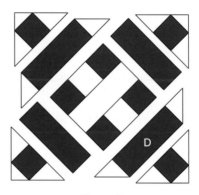

Figure 5
Arrange units as shown;
stitch to complete 1 block.

Red Print 1
Make 18

Strawberry Print 1
Make 12

Strawberry Print 2
Make 12

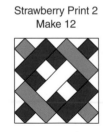

Figure 6
Make blocks as shown.

13. Arrange blocks in seven rows of six blocks each, arranging different fabric blocks as shown in Figure 7. Join blocks in rows; join

R	S1	S2	S1	S2	R
R	S2	S1	S2	S1	R
R	S1	S2	S1	S2	R
R	S2	S1	S2	S1	R
R	S1	S2	S1	S2	R
R	S2	S1	S2	S1	R
R	R	R	R	R	R

Figure 7
Arrange blocks as shown.
R = Red print 1
S1 = Strawberry print 1
S2 = Strawberry print 2

Strawberry Red Album
Placement Diagram
84" x 92½"

rows to complete pieced center. Press seams in one direction.

14. Cut and piece two border strips each 3" x 84½" and 3" x 77½" from strawberry print 3. Sew longer strips to opposite long sides and shorter strips to top and bottom of pieced center; press seams toward strips.

15. Cut and piece two long border strips 4" x 89½" and one strip 4" x 84½" from red print 2. Sew longer strips to opposite long sides and shorter strip to the bottom of pieced center; press seams toward strips. **Note:** *There is no red print border strip on the top of the quilt shown.*

16. Sandwich batting between the completed top and prepared backing piece; pin or baste to hold flat for quilting.

17. Quilt as desired by hand or machine.

18. Trim edges even. Bind edges with self-made or purchased binding to finish **Note:** *Binding for this quilt was made using one each 7"-wide strip white solid and strawberry prints 1 and 2. Join strips along long sides; cut into 2"-wide segments. Join on the short ends to make 10½ yards self-made binding.* ■

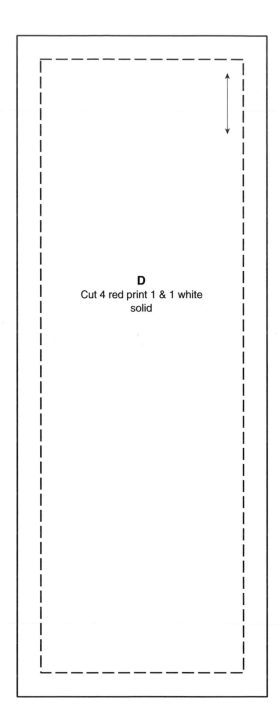

D
Cut 4 red print 1 & 1 white
solid

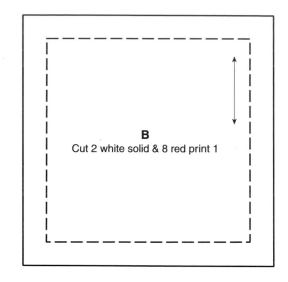

B
Cut 2 white solid & 8 red print 1

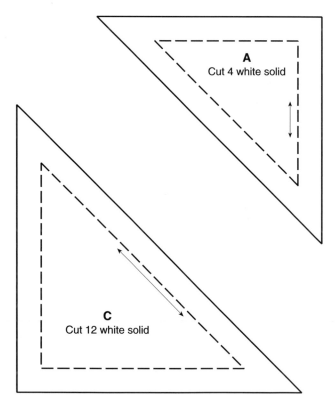

A
Cut 4 white solid

C
Cut 12 white solid

Old-Fashioned Sunshine

BY SANDRA L. HATCH

Every day will be sunny when you wrap up in this day-brightener of a quilt. This allover design is made with only two fabrics, the yellow being typical of a 1930s print.

Project Specifications
Skill Level: Advanced
Quilt Size: 72" x 87"
Unit Size: 7" x 7"

Fabric & Batting
- 2 yards solid white
- 5¼ yards yellow print
- Backing 74" x 89"
- Batting 74" x 89"
- 11 yards self-made or purchased binding

Supplies & Tools
- All-purpose thread to match fabrics
- Quilting thread
- Basic sewing supplies and tools and water-erasable marker or pencil

Project Note
By introducing more than two colors to this longtime favorite pattern, you will completely change the look of the quilt. Before you begin, experiment with colored pencils and photocopies of the Placement Diagram. You'll enjoy discovering creative ways to use some of your treasured fabric scraps.

Instructions
1. Piece units by sewing A to B as shown in Figure 1. Complete row units making two types of rows referring to Figure 2. You will need nine rows of 14 B squares and eight half-unit rows. Each crosswise row has 14 B pieces and each lengthwise row has 17 B pieces.

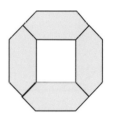

Old-Fashioned Sunshine
7" x 7" Unit

Figure 1
Sew A to B as shown.

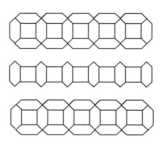

Figure 2
Join pieces to make rows instead of blocks as shown. Join whole-unit rows with half-unit rows as shown.

2. Arrange completed rows in sequence and join together to complete pieced top. Press.

3. Mark chosen quilting design on B squares using a water-erasable marker or pencil. The design used on the quilt shown is marked in dotted lines on B. The A pieces are quilted ¼" and ½" in from seams on each piece.

4. Sandwich batting between completed top and prepared backing piece; pin or baste layers together to hold flat. Quilt as desired by hand or machine.

5. Trim edges even; bind with self-made or purchased binding to finish. ■

Old-Fashioned Sunshine
Placement Diagram
72" x 87"

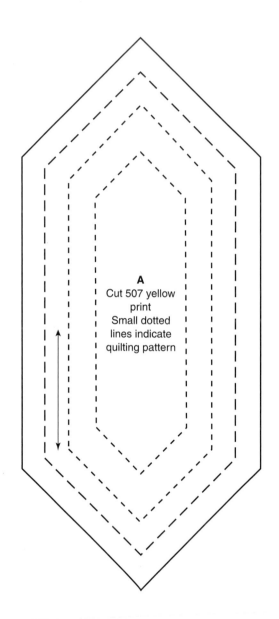

A
Cut 507 yellow print
Small dotted lines indicate quilting pattern

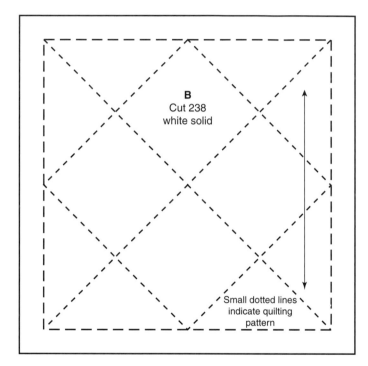

B
Cut 238 white solid

Small dotted lines indicate quilting pattern

Thanksgiving

BY CONNIE RAND

Thanksgiving is a time to thank God for the blessings in our lives. Make this pretty table cover using a Thanksgiving print to share your love of quilting during your family gathering.

Project Specifications
Skill Level: Advanced beginner
Quilt Size: 64" x 80"
Block Size: 16" x 16"
Number of Blocks: 20

Fabric & Batting
- 2¾ yards Thanksgiving print
- 1¾ yards cream-on-cream print
- 1¾ yards dark green solid
- Batting 68" x 84"
- Backing 68" x 84"
- 8½ yards self-made or purchased binding

Supplies & Tools
- Neutral color all-purpose thread
- Basic sewing tools and supplies

Piecing Blocks

1. Prepare templates using pattern pieces given. Cut as directed on each piece for one block; repeat for 20 blocks.

2. Referring to Figure 1, sew a dark green A square between two Thanksgiving print A squares. Sew a dark green C to a Thanksgiving print C. Sew a cream-on-cream print C to each side. Repeat for four C units.

Thanksgiving
16" x 16" Block

3. Sew the C unit to B. Repeat for four B-C units. Sew a Thanksgiving print A between two B-C units. Repeat.

4. Sew the A unit made in step 2 between two B-C units made in step 3 to make the center of the block.

Figure 1
Piece block as shown.

5. Sew a green DR to E to a Thanksgiving print D to E to a Thanksgiving print DR to E to a Thanksgiving print D to make side units; repeat for four units. Sew side units to pieced center to complete one block; repeat for 20 blocks.

6. Sew blocks together in four rows of five blocks each referring to the Placement Diagram.

7. Sandwich batting between completed top and prepared backing piece; pin or baste layers together to hold flat. Quilt as desired by hand or machine.

8. Trim edges even; bind with self-made or purchased binding to finish. ◼

Thanksgiving
Placement Diagram
64" x 80"

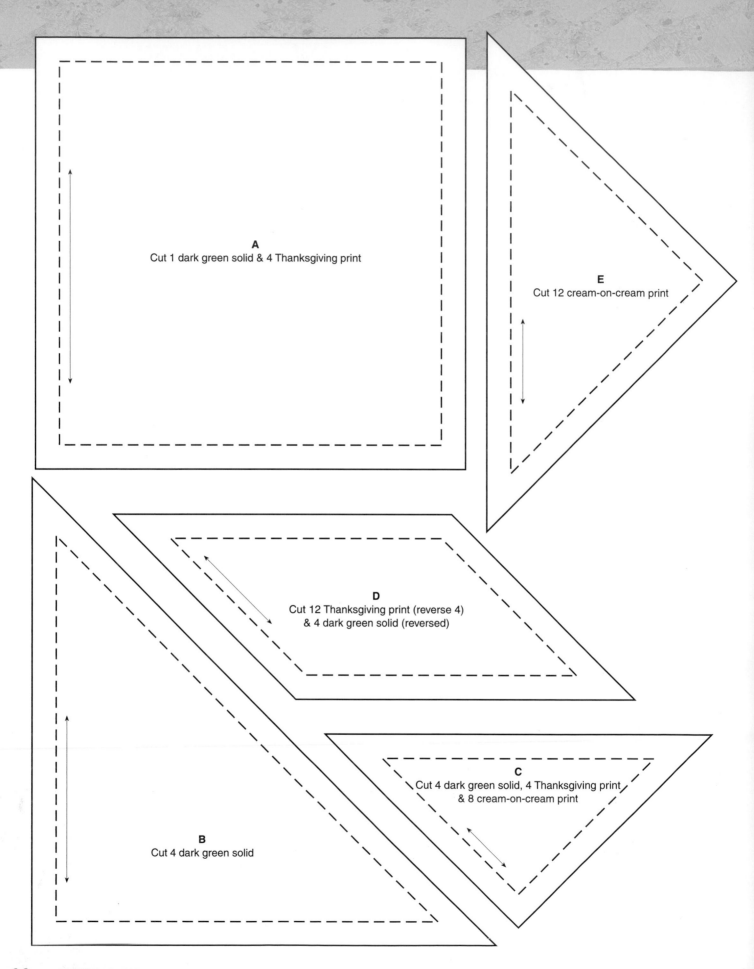

A
Cut 1 dark green solid & 4 Thanksgiving print

E
Cut 12 cream-on-cream print

D
Cut 12 Thanksgiving print (reverse 4)
& 4 dark green solid (reversed)

C
Cut 4 dark green solid, 4 Thanksgiving print
& 8 cream-on-cream print

B
Cut 4 dark green solid

Tree of Life

BY HELEN KING

This quilt will look great on your bed every day of the year, but especially at Christmastime.

Project Specifications
Skill Level: Advanced
Quilt Size: 70" x 62"
Block Size: 14" x 14"

Fabric & Batting
- 4½ yards white solid
- 3¾ yards green solid or print
- Backing 66" x 74"
- Batting 66" x 74"
- 7½ yards self-made or purchased binding

Supplies & Tools
- All-purpose thread to match fabrics
- Quilting thread
- Basic sewing supplies and tools, and water-erasable marker or pencil

Instructions
Traditional Method

1. Prepare templates using pattern pieces given. Cut as directed on each piece for one block. Repeat for 16 blocks.

2. To piece one block, sew 19 white and green A triangles together to make squares. Arrange these with the remaining pieces as shown in Figure 1; join to complete one block. Repeat for 16 blocks; press and square up to 14½" x 14½".

3. Cut nine sashing squares 2½" x 2½" from white.

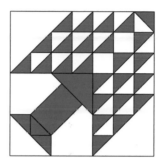

Tree of Life
14" x 14" Block

4. Cut 24 sashing strips 2½" x 14½" from green.

5. Join four blocks with three green sashing strips; repeat for four rows. Press seams toward strips.

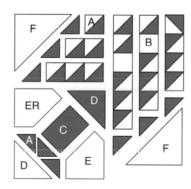

Figure 1
Join triangle/squares with other pieces as shown to make 1 block.

6. Join four sashing strips with three sashing squares to make a row as shown in Figure 2; repeat for three rows.

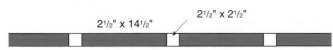

Figure 2
Join 4 sashing strips with 3 sashing squares as shown.

7. Arrange block rows with sashing rows; sew together to complete center section of top.

8. Cut two strips each green and white 2½" x 62½". Sew to sides; press seams toward strips.

9. Mark the completed top with a chosen quilting design using a water-erasable marker or pencil.

10. Sandwich batting between completed top and prepared backing piece. Baste or pin layers together.

11. Quilt on marked lines or as desired by hand or machine.

12. When quilting is complete, trim edges even. Bind with self-made or purchased binding to finish.

Quicker Method
1. Cut 11 strips white and 17 green 2⅞" by fabric width.

2. Layer a green strip with a white strip; cut into 2⅞" segments. Repeat to make 11 green/white strips.

3. Mark a diagonal line from corner to corner on the white square side. Sew ¼" on each side of

the line; cut apart along drawn line to make two triangle/square sets as shown in Figure 3. You will need 304 white/green sets to complete the quilt as shown.

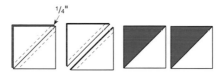

Figure 3
Place a white square and a green square right sides together; mark the diagonal. Sew ¼" on each side of the diagonal line; cut on the diagonal line to make 2 triangle/squares.

4. Cut the six remaining green print strips into 2⅞" segments. Cut each segment in half on the diagonal to make A triangles.

5. Cut two strips green 3⁵⁄₁₆" by fabric width. Cut strips into 4¾" segments for piece C. You will need 16 C pieces.

6. Cut three strips white solid 6⅞" by fabric width. Cut each strip into 6⅞" segments. Cut each segment in half on the diagonal for F triangles.

7. Cut one strip each white and green 4⅞" by fabric width. Cut each strip into 4⅞" segments. Cut each segment in half on the diagonal for D triangles.

8. Cut E pieces using template as directed.

9. Finish blocks and quilt as for Traditional Method. ■

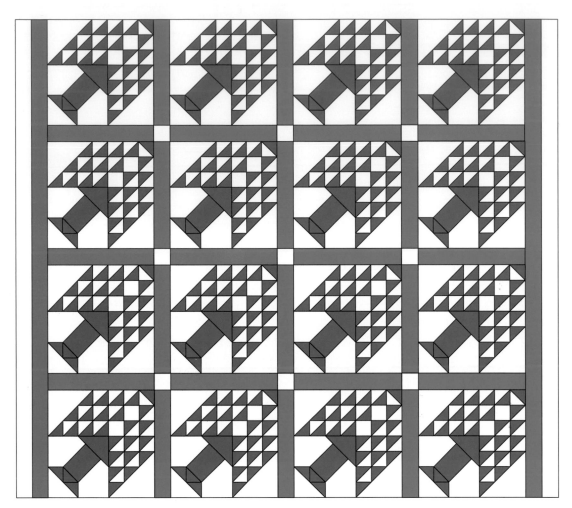

Tree of Life Quilt
Placement Diagram
70" x 62"

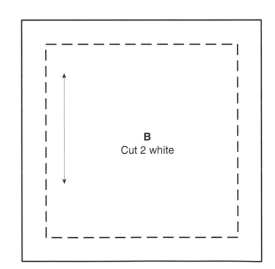

A
Cut 19 white & 28 green

B
Cut 2 white

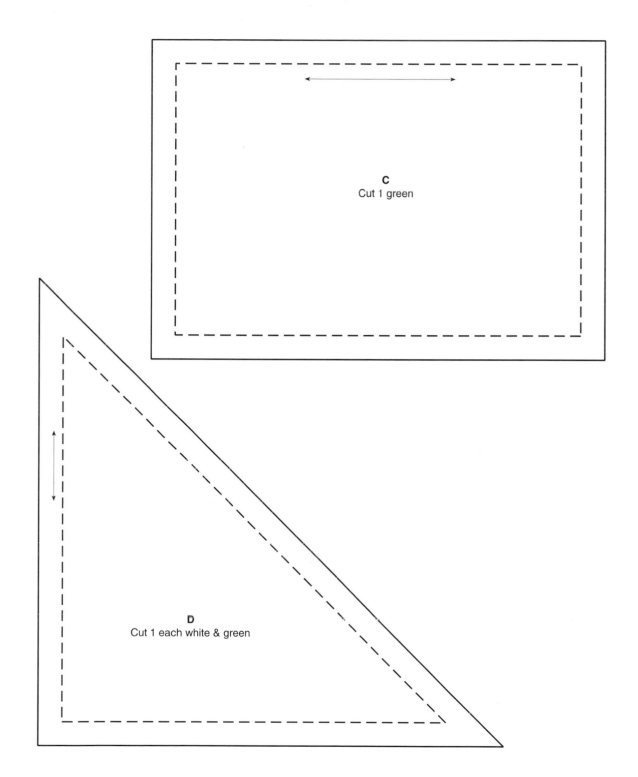

C
Cut 1 green

D
Cut 1 each white & green

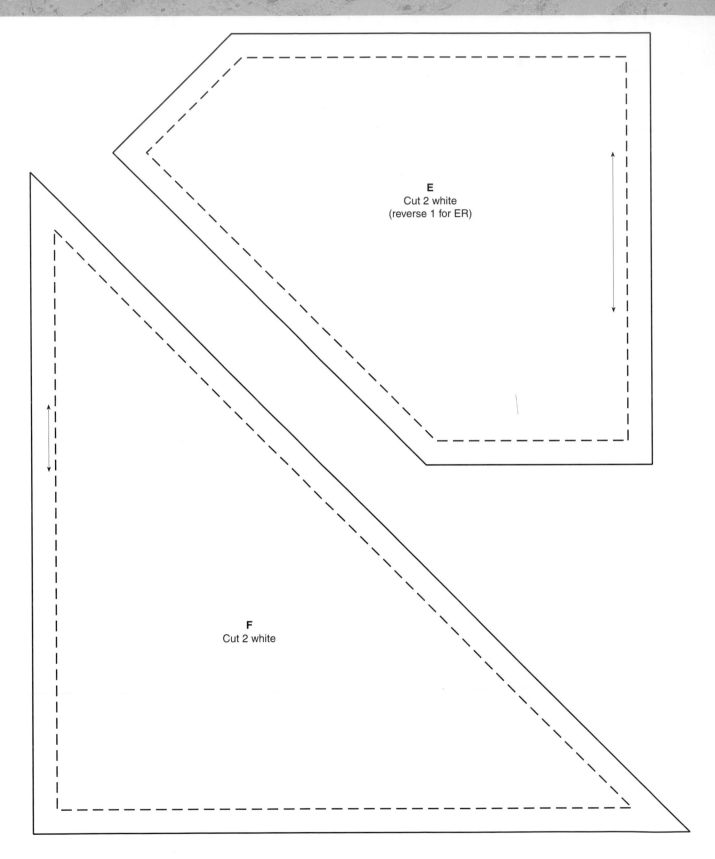

E
Cut 2 white
(reverse 1 for ER)

F
Cut 2 white

Dream Catcher Delight

BY LUCY A. FAZELY & MICHAEL L. BURNS

Capture all the good in your dreams while the bad escapes through the hole in the center of this dream-catcher design.

Project Specifications

Skill Level: Beginner
Quilt Size: 76" x 92"
Block Size: 16" x 16"
Number of Blocks: 20

Materials

- ½ yard navy solid
- ½ yard pale blue solid
- ⅝ yard light blue solid
- ⅝ yard medium blue solid
- 3 yards navy print
- 4¾ yards white solid
- Batting 82" x 98"
- Backing 82" x 98"

Supplies & Tools

- Neutral color all-purpose thread
- Clear nylon monofilament
- White quilting thread
- 11 yards 12"-wide fusible web
- 8½ yards 20"-wide tear-off fabric stabilizer
- Basic sewing tools and supplies

Instructions

1. Prepare templates for appliqué shapes using patterns given.

Dream Catcher
16" x 16" Block

2. Bond fusible web to the wrong side of ¾ yard navy print and all of the remaining fabrics.

3. Trace appliqué shapes on the paper side of the fused fabrics referring to patterns for color and number to cut of each shape. Cut out shapes on traced lines; remove paper backing.

4. Cut 20 white solid A squares 16½" x 16½"; fold and crease each square to mark vertical, horizontal and diagonal centers as shown in Figure 1.

Figure 1
Fold and crease each
A square to mark
vertical, horizontal
and diagonal centers.

5. Center and pin an F piece on an A square using crease lines as guides for placement. Arrange one E and two each B, C and D pieces on diagonal spokes of F as shown in Figure 2, tucking ends under F; fuse shapes in place. Repeat for 20 blocks.

Figure 2
Arrange 1 E and 2 each
B, C and D pieces on
diagonal spokes of F.

6. Cut 20 squares tear-off fabric stabilizer 15" x 15"; pin a square to the wrong side of each fused block.

7. Machine-appliqué around edges of each fused piece using clear nylon monofilament in the top

of the machine and all-purpose thread in the bobbin and a narrow machine zigzag stitch.

8. When appliqué stitching is complete, remove stabilizer.

9. Join four blocks to make a row; press seams in one direction; repeat for five rows.

10. Join the rows to complete the pieced center; press seams in one direction.

11. Cut and piece two 6½" x 76½" G strips and two 6½" x 80½" H strips navy print. Sew H to opposite long sides and G to the top and bottom of the pieced center; press seams toward strips.

Finishing the Quilt

1. Sandwich batting between the completed top and prepared backing piece; pin or baste layers together to hold flat for quilting.

2. Quilt as desired by hand or machine. ***Note:** The quilt shown was professionally machine-quilted around appliqué shapes and in a patterned cable design on borders using white quilting thread.*

3. When quilting is complete, trim batting and backing even with quilted top; remove pins or basting.

4. Cut nine 2¼" by fabric width strips navy print; join strips on short ends to make one long strip for binding.

5. Fold the binding strip in half along length with wrong sides together; press.

6. Bind edges to finish. ■

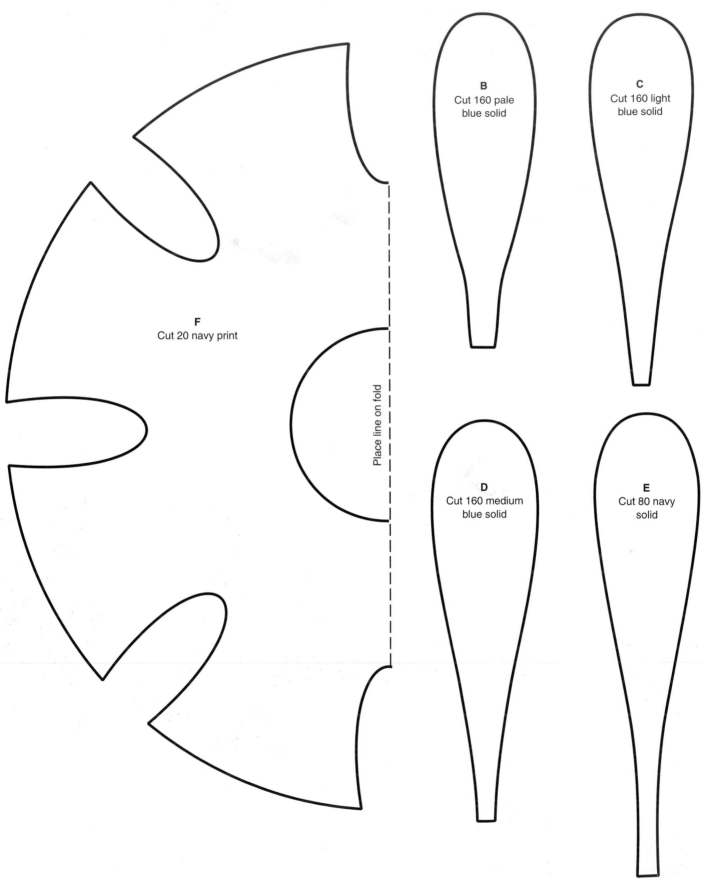

B
Cut 160 pale
blue solid

C
Cut 160 light
blue solid

F
Cut 20 navy print

Place line on fold

D
Cut 160 medium
blue solid

E
Cut 80 navy
solid

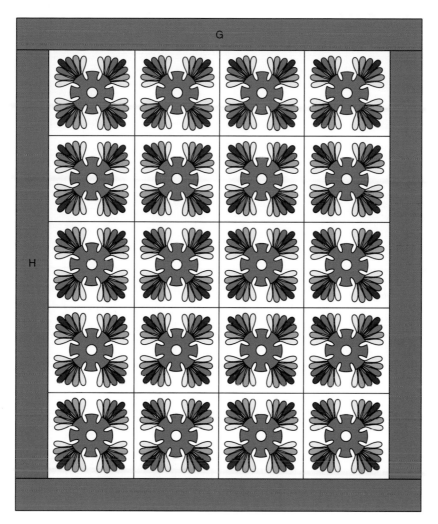

Dream Catcher Delight
Placement Diagram
76" x 92"

True Lover's Knot

BY SANDRA L. HATCH

This blue-and-white quilt is a copy of an antique quilt from the late 1880s.

Project Specifications
Skill Level: Beginner
Quilt Size: 78" x 78"
Block Size: 13½" x 13½"
Number of Blocks: 16

Fabric & Batting
- 4¼ yards navy blue print
- 4½ yards white solid
- Backing 82" x 82"
- Batting 82" x 82"
- 8¾ yards self-made or purchased binding

Supplies & Tools
- White all-purpose thread
- Quilting thread
- Basic sewing supplies and tools

Project Note
Today the way the blocks are put together and the border treatment on this quilt would be changed. An alternative design would be to have smaller blocks in each border corner and navy blue sashing squares with white solid sashing strips between blocks. If these changes are appealing to you, see Figure 1 for placement.

Instructions
1. Cut 25 strips navy blue print and 29 strips white solid 2" by fabric width.

2. Sew a white strip to a navy strip to a white strip;

True Lover's Knot
13½" x 13½" Block

Figure 1
A better design is formed when dark sashing squares or Nine-Patch blocks are placed at the block corners in the sashing. Border corners would also look better with a block in the corner.

press seams toward the navy strip. Repeat for 11 strip sets. Cut three strip sets into 2" segments

and eight strip sets into 5" segments referring to Figure 2.

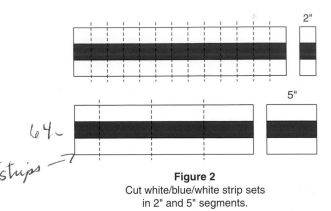

Figure 2
Cut white/blue/white strip sets in 2" and 5" segments.

(handwritten notes: "64", "make 11 strips")

3. Sew a navy strip to a white strip to a navy strip; press seams toward the navy strips. Repeat for seven strip sets. Cut each strip into 2" segments.

4. Sew a white/navy/white segment between two navy/white/navy segments to complete one Nine-Patch unit as shown in Figure 3. Repeat for 64 units.

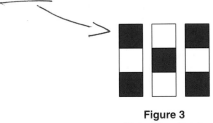

Figure 3
Make Nine-Patch units as shown.

5. Cut two strips 5" by fabric width navy blue print. Cut strips into 5" segments. You will need 16 segments.

6. Arrange the stitched units in rows with a 5" segment as shown in Figure 4. Join units in rows; join rows to complete one block. Press; repeat for 16 blocks.

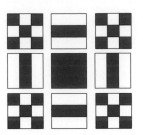

Figure 4
Arrange stitched units in rows to make 1 block.

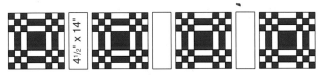

Figure 5
Join 4 blocks with 3 strips.

7. Cut 12 strips white 4½" x 14". Join four blocks with three strips to make one row as shown in Figure 5; press seams toward strips. Repeat for four rows.

8. Cut three strips 4½" x 66½" white solid. Join the block rows with these strips to complete pieced center.

9. Cut two strips navy 2" x 66½" and four strips white 2¾" x 66½". Sew a navy strip between two white strips; press seams toward navy. Repeat for a second strip. Sew a pieced strip to opposite sides of the quilt center.

10. Cut two strips navy 2" x 78½" and four strips white 2¾" x 78½". Sew strips together as in step 9 and sew to top and bottom of quilt center; press seams toward strips.

11. Mark sashing strips with quilting designs given referring to the Placement Diagram for arrangement. Mark border strips with straight lines perpendicular to the quilt center for quilting.

12. Sandwich batting between completed top and prepared backing piece; pin or baste layers together to hold flat. Quilt as desired by hand or machine.

13. Trim edges even; bind with self-made or purchased binding to finish. ■

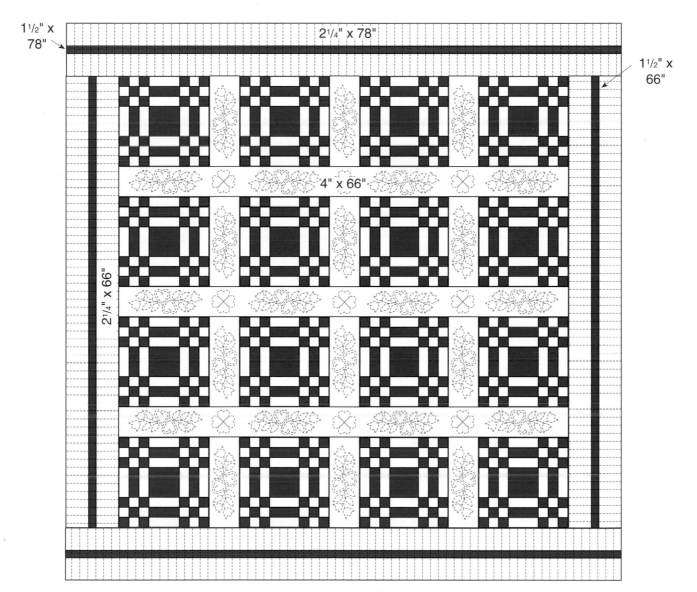

True Lover's Knot
Placement Diagram
78" x 78"

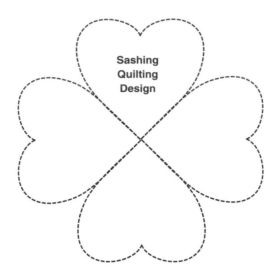

Sashing
Quilting
Design

Sashing Quilting Design

Four-Patch Diamonds

BY CONNIE RAND

Gradations of blue are featured in this quilt, but if you prefer, use shades of your favorite color instead.

Project Specifications

Skill Level: Intermediate
Quilt Size: 55" x 71"
Block Size: 12" x 16"
Number of Blocks: 16

Fabric & Batting

- ⅔ yard medium blue print (blue print 5)
- ⅞ yard light medium blue print (blue print 2)
- 1⅛ yards navy solid
- 1⅛ yards lightest blue print (blue print 1)
- 1¼ yards dark medium blue print (blue print 3)
- 2 yards darkest blue print for blocks and borders (blue print 4)
- Batting 60" x 76"
- Backing 60" x 76"
- 7½ yards self-made or purchased binding

Supplies & Tools

- Coordinating all-purpose thread
- Rotary cutter, mat and ruler
- Basic sewing supplies and tools

Instructions

1. Cut two strips 4" x 48½" and two strips 4" x 64½" blue print 4 from fabric length for borders; set aside.

2. Prepare templates using pattern pieces given. Cut as directed on each piece for one block; repeat for 16 blocks.

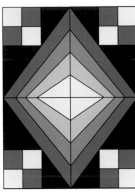

Four-Patch Diamonds
12" x 16" Block

3. Join four G pieces to make a Four-Patch unit in colors shown in Figure 1.

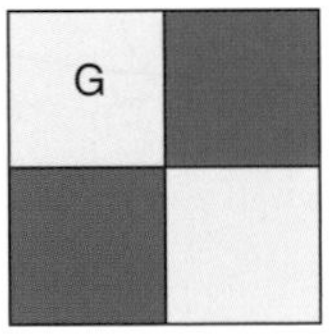

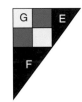

Figure 1
Sew G pieces together as shown to make a Four-Patch unit.

Figure 2
Sew E and F to the pieced Four-Patch unit.

4. Sew A to B to C to D. Sew E to the previously pieced Four-Patch unit, referring to Figure 2; add F. Sew the E-F-G unit to A-B-C-D to complete one quarter of the block; repeat for two sections.

HOUSE OF WHITE BIRCHES, BERNE, INDIANA 46711   WWW.WHITEBIRCHES.COM

Sew reverse pieces together in same sequence, repeating for two sections. Assemble the block referring to Figure 3; press. Repeat for 16 blocks.

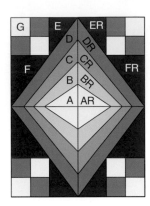

Figure 3
Sew block quarters together as
shown to complete 1 block.

5. Sew blocks together in four rows of four blocks each to complete quilt center. Press seams in one direction.

6. Stitch four Four-Patch border units with G referring to Figure 1.

7. Sew 4" x 48½" strips cut in step 1 to the top and bottom of the pieced center; press seams toward strips. Sew a Four-Patch unit to each end of each 4" x 64½" strip; sew to opposite sides. Press seams toward strips.

8. Sandwich batting between the completed top and prepared backing piece; pin or baste layers together to hold flat for quilting.

9. Quilt as desired by hand or machine.

10. Bind edges with self-made or purchased binding to finish. ■

COLOR KEY
- ☐ Blue print 1
- ☐ Blue print 2
- ☐ Blue print 3
- ☐ Blue print 4
- ☐ Blue print 5
- ■ Navy solid

3½" x 48"

3½" x 64"

Four-Patch Diamonds
Placement Diagram
55" x 71"

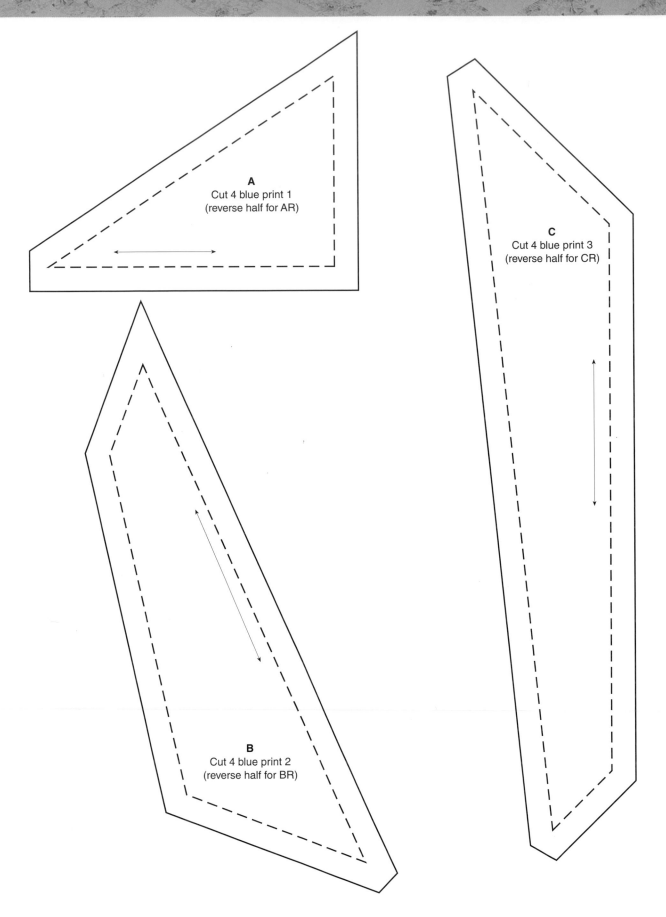

A
Cut 4 blue print 1
(reverse half for AR)

C
Cut 4 blue print 3
(reverse half for CR)

B
Cut 4 blue print 2
(reverse half for BR)

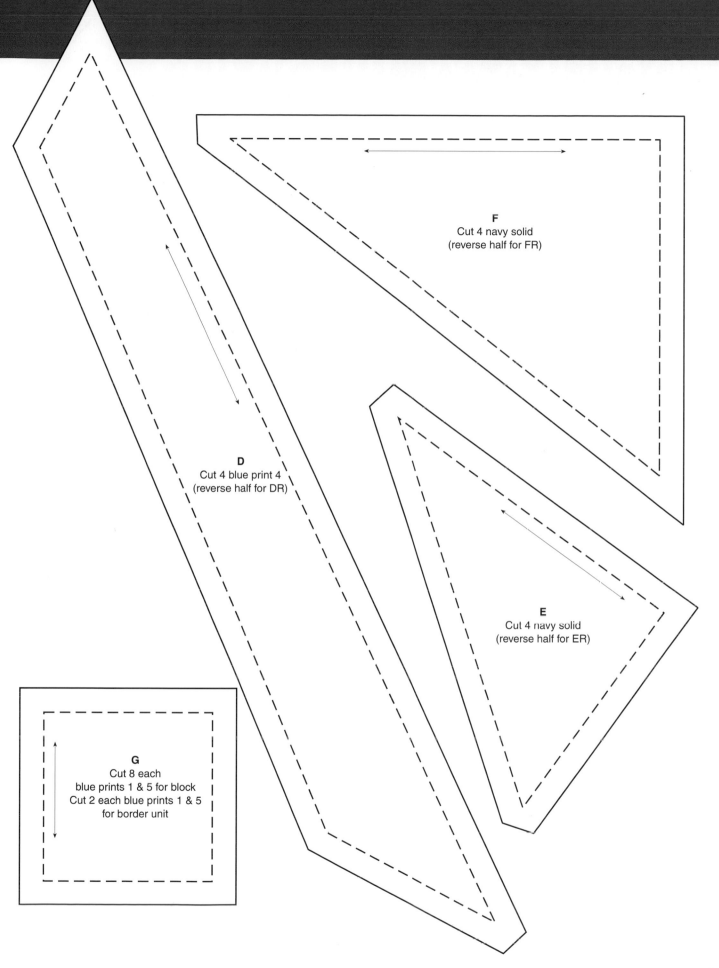

F
Cut 4 navy solid
(reverse half for FR)

D
Cut 4 blue print 4
(reverse half for DR)

E
Cut 4 navy solid
(reverse half for ER)

G
Cut 8 each
blue prints 1 & 5 for block
Cut 2 each blue prints 1 & 5
for border unit

Rainbow Illusions

BY LUCY A. FAZELY

Use fat quarters in a rainbow of colors to create this festive quilt, similar to the Log Cabin barn-raising design.

Project Specifications
Skill Level: Intermediate
Quilt Size: 48" x 58" (68" x 88" or 88" x 108")
Block Size: 5" x 5"
Number of Blocks: 28 (64 or 108)

Fabric & Batting
- 6 (14 or 22) fat quarters white prints
- 6 (14 or 22) fat quarters colored prints
- 1¼ (1¾ or 2¼) yards border and binding fabric
- Backing 52" x 62" (72" x 92" or 94" x 114")
- Batting 52" x 62" (72" x 92" or 94" x 114")

Supplies & Tools
- Coordinating all-purpose thread
- Quilting thread
- Basic sewing supplies and tools

Project Notes
Instructions are given to make three sizes of this quilt. The amounts listed in parentheses in the Project Specifications, Fabric and Batting and in the Instructions are for the alternate sizes. Quilt in photo is 68" x 88".

If you choose to use a different number of fabrics than listed, remember to purchase the same total yardage. For example, if you use 20 fabrics instead of 12, you still need a total of 1½ (3½ or 5½) yards of colored fabrics to complete the quilt.

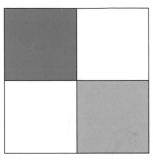

Four-Patch
5" x 5" Block

Instructions
Note: From each fat quarter it is possible to cut either one strip 5⅞" x 22" and three strips 3" x 22" or two strips 5⅞" x 22" and one strip 3" x 22". It doesn't matter which choice you make for each fat quarter as long as you have the right total number of colored and white strips as listed.

1. From both the white and colored fat quarters cut nine (22 or 36) strips 5⅞" x 22" and 10 (22 or 36) strips 3" x 22". **Note:** Extra 3"-wide strips are cut to result in a more random color placement in the quilt.

2. Cut 5⅞" strips into 5⅞" segments to make squares; you will need 26 (64 or 106) squares each white and colored.

3. Mark a diagonal line from corner to corner on the wrong side of each white square. Draw a line ¼" on each side of the first line as shown in Figure 1.

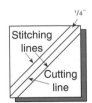

Figure 1
Draw a line ¼" away from
diagonal line on both sides.

4. Place each white square right sides together with a colored square. Stitch on both ¼" lines as shown in Figure 2. Repeat for all 5⅞" x 5⅞" squares.

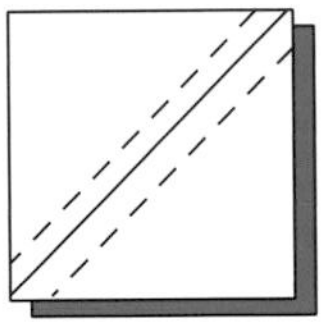

Figure 2
Stitch on marked ¼" lines.

5. Cut each stitched square along diagonal line; trim excess seam at corners as shown in Figure 3. Open stitched unit to reveal a triangle/square as shown in Figure 4. Press seams toward colored triangle.

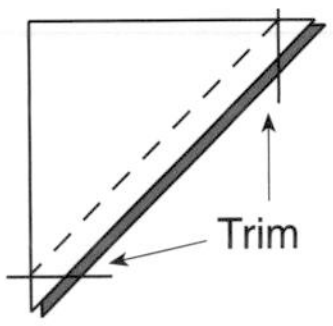

Figure 3
Trim excess at corners.

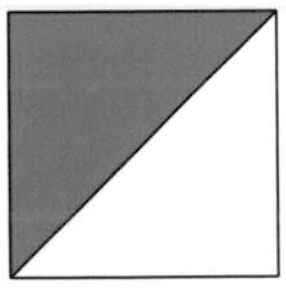

Figure 4
Open to reveal a
triangle/square.

6. Join a 3" x 22" white strip with a 3" x 22" colored strip along 22" side; press seams toward colored strip. Repeat for 10 (22 or 36) strip sets. Cut each strip set into 3" segments. Randomly choose 56 (128 or 216) segments for use in the blocks.

7. Join two segments to make a Four-Patch block as shown in Figure 5; press seams in one direction. Repeat for 28 (64 or 108) Four-Patch blocks.

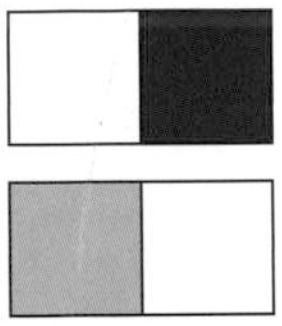

Figure 5
Join 2 segments to make a
Four-Patch block.

8. On a flat surface, lay out all triangle/squares with Four-Patch blocks referring to the Placement Diagram for arrangement of blocks. **Note:** *The darker black lines on the Placement Diagram separate the different sizes of quilts. The inside dark line indicates the 48" x 58" quilt, the next dark line indicates the 68" x 88" quilt, and the largest outside line indicates the 88" x 108" quilt.*

9. Join blocks together in rows; press. Join rows together to complete pieced center; press.

10. Cut six (eight or 10) strips 4½" x 44" for borders. Cut and join strips on short ends to make two strips 50½" (80½" or 100½") and two strips 48½" (68½" or 88½").

11. Sew the longer strips to opposite long sides of the pieced center and the shorter strips to the top and bottom; press seams toward strips.

12. Sandwich batting between the completed top and prepared backing piece; pin or baste layers together to hold flat. Quilt as desired by hand or machine.

13. Trim edges even. Prepare 6 (9 or 11) yards self-made binding using border fabric. Bind edges to finish. ■

Rainbow Illusions
Placement Diagram
48" x 58"
(68" x 88" & 88" x 108")

Log Cabin Color Blocks

BY JOYCE MORI

Your choice of fabric and the placement of color blocks will make this quilt uniquely yours. Have fun experimenting with colors.

Project Specifications
Skill Level: Beginner
Quilt Size: 57" x 66½"
Block Size: 9½" x 9½"
Number of Blocks: 42

Fabric & Batting
- ⅓ yard red solid
- Scraps or fat quarters of the following color fabrics: light and dark blue; light and dark purple; light and dark red; light, medium and dark green; light and medium gray; black; yellow; orange; and peach
- Backing 61" x 70"
- Batting 61" x 70"
- 7½ yards self-made or purchased binding

Supplies & Tools
- All-purpose thread to match fabrics
- Quilting thread
- Rotary cutter, mat and ruler
- Basic sewing supplies and tools

Project Notes
The method of construction for these blocks is a bit different due to the experimentation with colors.

Begin by making copies of the line drawing for this quilt in Figure 1. The line drawing is done in triangles rather than pieced Log Cabin blocks. The triangle drawing allows you to see how you can color in squares of color. If you look at a block you can see that it is divided in half with

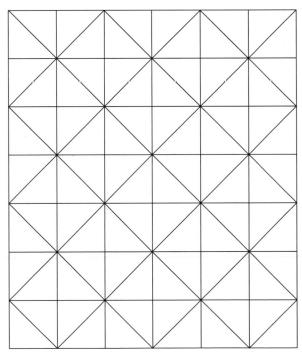

Figure 1
Copy the drawing as shown; color triangles to make design.

a different color in each half. One half of the square has a dark color and the other half a light color. Placement of the colors is arbitrary; do what you find pleasing.

If you color in the line drawing first, you will have a plan for sewing the blocks. You can make some squares more prominent by using some very dark fabrics, or you can make the squares fade in and out by using some medium fabrics.

The squares in this quilt do not always stand out because the designer used some medium-value fabrics. If you want a more planned formal look, position the dark squares carefully and use dark fabrics along the outside edges. The center square in this quilt block is always red and provides a constant in the design.

This pattern is a variation of the Sunshine and Shadows design; however, in the traditional coloring of the design the center squares are colored so they are very distinct.

Instructions

1. Cut three strips red solid 2½" by fabric width; cut each strip into 2½" segments. You will need 42 segments for centers.

2. Sort through your fabrics. Rotary-cut a wide selection of light and dark strips 1¾" wide in a wide range of your fabrics.

3. Referring to Figure 1, color triangles in your selected fabric colors. The triangles reflect half of a Log Cabin block. Figure 2 shows the color arrangement used for the quilt shown. Figure 5 shows how many blocks of each color are needed to make the quilt as shown. If you change colors, use these drawings as guides to create the number of blocks needed to complete the quilt as you have drawn it.

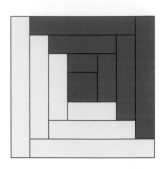

Log Cabin Color Blocks
9½" x 9½" Block

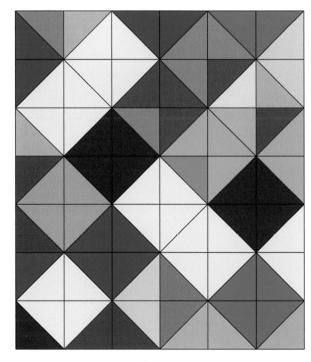

Figure 2
The quilt shown in the photo and Placement Diagram looks like this when Figure 1 is colored in.

4. To construct blocks, begin in the center with a 2½" red segment. Add the first two logs to the center square as shown in Figure 3 referring to Figure 5 for color arrangement of each type of block or to your own drawings for your color version.

5. Continue adding logs 3 and 4 referring to Figure 4. Complete all of one block combination color block before starting another color. For example, make two yellow/green blocks before starting the two yellow/blue blocks.

Figure 3
Sew logs 1 and 2 to the center square.

Figure 4
Continue adding logs 3 and 4.

6. As you sew, iron the seam allowance toward the newly added log and trim off the strip even with the previous segment.

7. Check off the blocks as you complete them in Figure 5 or in your own drawings.

8. Complete 42 blocks; press and square blocks to 10" x 10".

9. Arrange blocks in six rows of seven blocks each referring to the Placement Diagram. Join blocks in rows; press seams in adjoining rows in opposite directions. Join rows to complete the pieced top; press seams in one direction.

10. Sandwich batting between completed top and prepared backing piece. Safety-pin or baste layers together to hold flat. Quilt as desired by hand or machine.

11. Trim edges even; bind with self-made or purchased binding to finish. ■

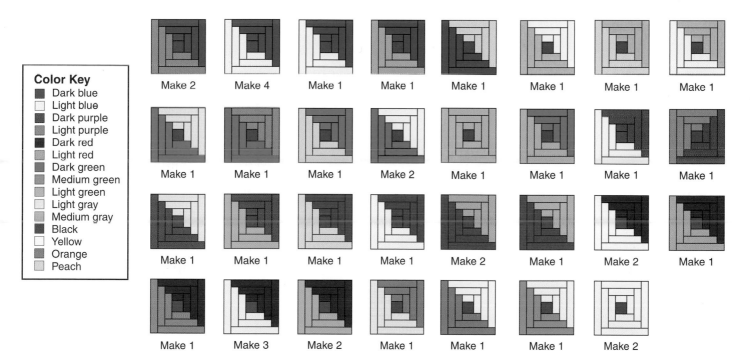

Color Key
- Dark blue
- Light blue
- Dark purple
- Light purple
- Dark red
- Light red
- Dark green
- Medium green
- Light green
- Light gray
- Medium gray
- Black
- Yellow
- Orange
- Peach

Make 2   Make 4   Make 1   Make 1   Make 1   Make 1   Make 1   Make 1

Make 1   Make 1   Make 1   Make 2   Make 1   Make 1   Make 1   Make 1

Make 1   Make 1   Make 1   Make 1   Make 2   Make 1   Make 2   Make 1

Make 1   Make 3   Make 2   Make 1   Make 1   Make 1   Make 2

Figure 5
Complete blocks in colors and numbers shown to make quilt shown in the photo and Placement Diagram.

Color Key
- Dark blue
- Light blue
- Dark purple
- Light purple
- Dark red
- Light red
- Dark green
- Medium green
- Light green
- Light gray
- Medium gray
- Black
- Yellow
- Orange
- Peach

Log Cabin Color Blocks
Placement Diagram
57" x 66½"

Embroidery Stitch Guide

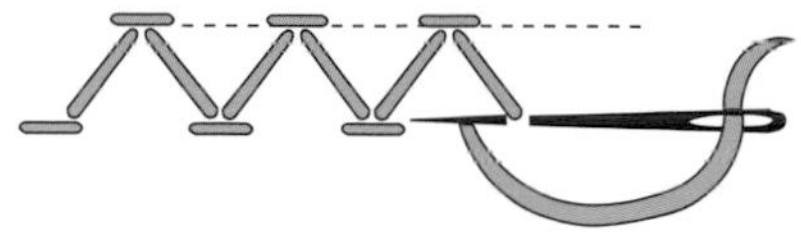

Chevron Stitch

Fly Stitch

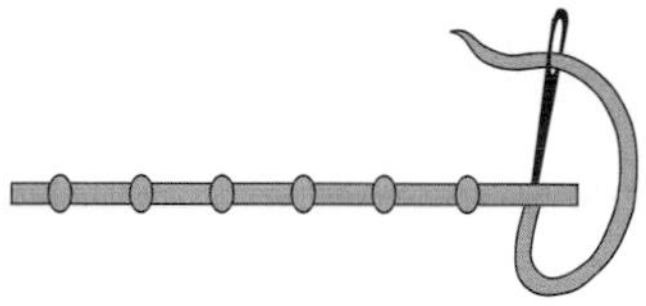

Couching Stitch

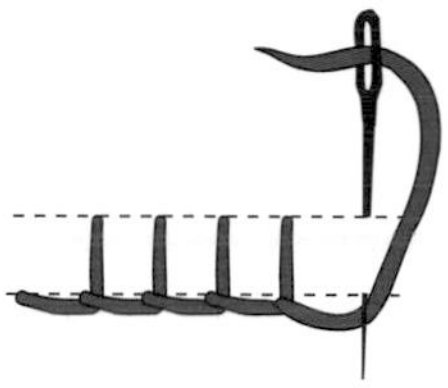

Buttonhole Stitch

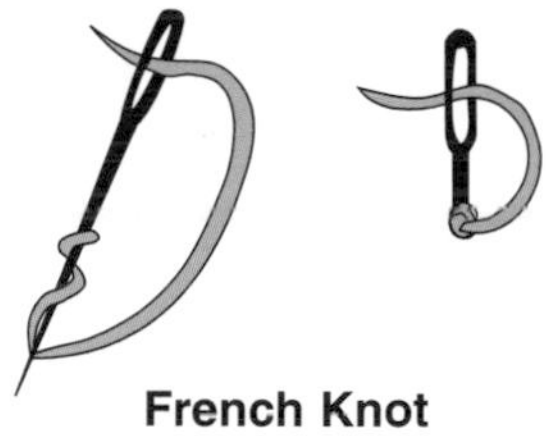

French Knot

Stem Stitch

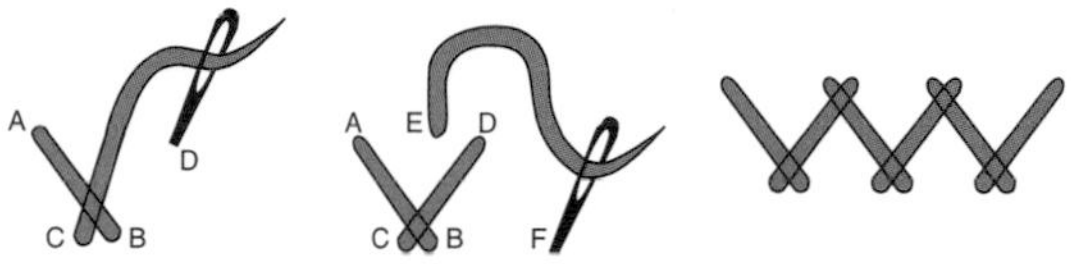

Herringbone Stitch

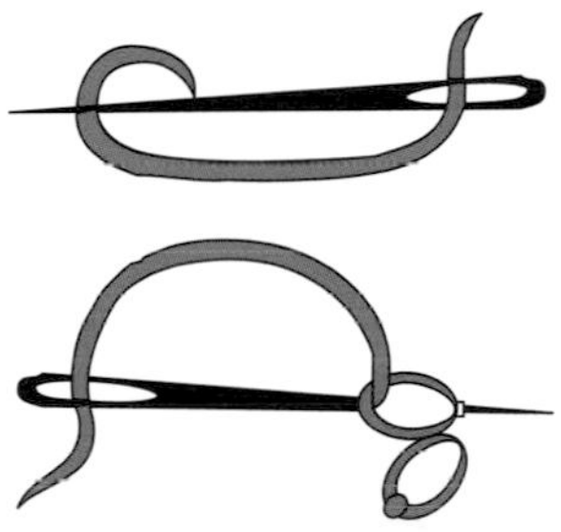

A   D   A E D

C B   C B F

Lazy Daisy Stitch

Chain Stitch

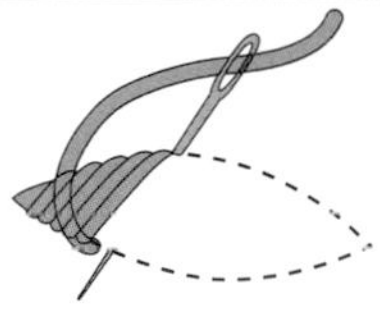

Satin Stitch

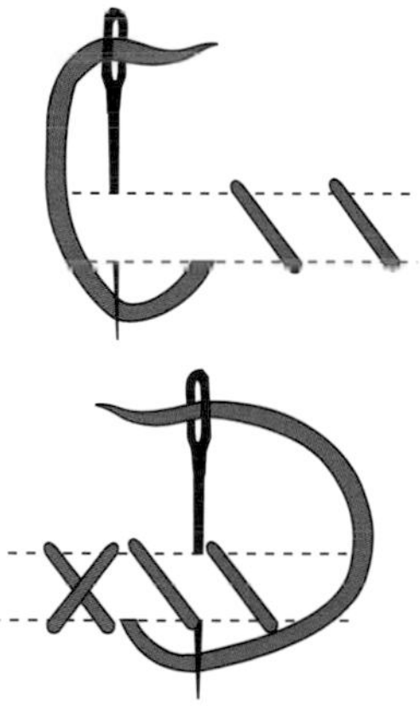

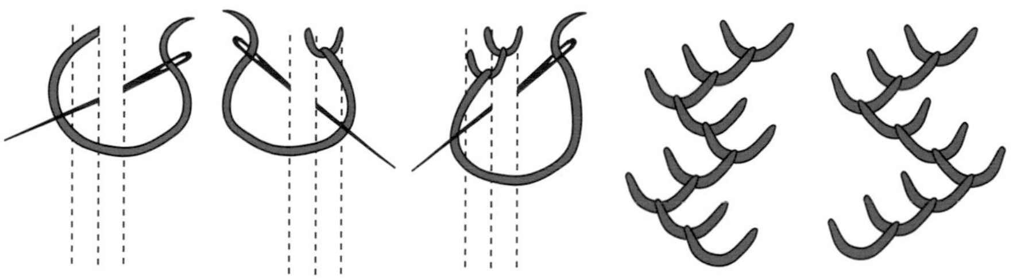

Feather Stitches

Cross-Stitch

Metric Conversion Charts

Metric Conversions

U.S. Measurement		Multiplied by		Metric Measurement
yards	x	.9144	=	meters (m)
yards	x	91.44	=	centimeters (cm)
inches	x	2.54	=	centimeters (cm)
inches	x	25.40	=	millimeters (mm)
inches	x	.0254	=	meters (m)

Metric Measurement		Multiplied by		U.S. Measurement
centimeters	x	.3937	=	inches
meters	x	1.0936	=	yards

Standard Equivalents

U.S. Measurement		Metric Measurement		
1/8 inch	=	3.20 mm	=	0.32 cm
1/4 inch	=	6.35 mm	=	0.635 cm
3/8 inch	=	9.50 mm	=	0.95 cm
1/2 inch	=	12.70 mm	=	1.27 cm
5/8 inch	=	15.90 mm	=	1.59 cm
3/4 inch	=	19.10 mm	=	1.91 cm
7/8 inch	=	22.20 mm	=	2.22 cm
1 inch	=	25.40 mm	=	2.54 cm
1/8 yard	=	11.43 cm	=	0.11 m
1/4 yard	=	22.86 cm	=	0.23 m
3/8 yard	=	34.29 cm	=	0.34 m
1/2 yard	=	45.72 cm	=	0.46 m
5/8 yard	=	57.15 cm	=	0.57 m
3/4 yard	=	68.58 cm	=	0.69 m
7/8 yard	=	80.00 cm	=	0.80 m
1 yard	=	91.44 cm	=	0.91 m

U.S. Measurement		Metric Measurement		
1 1/8 yard	=	102.87 cm	=	1.03 m
1 1/4 yard	=	114.30 cm	=	1.14 m
1 3/8 yard	=	125.73 cm	=	1.26 m
1 1/2 yard	=	137.16 cm	=	1.37 m
1 5/8 yard	=	148.59 cm	=	1.49 m
1 3/4 yard	=	160.02 cm	=	1.60 m
1 7/8 yard	=	171.44 cm	=	1.71 m
2 yards	=	182.88 cm	=	1.83 m
2 1/8 yards	=	194.31 cm	=	1.94 m
2 1/4 yards	=	205.74 cm	=	2.06 m
2 3/8 yards	=	217.17 cm	=	2.17 m
2 1/2 yards	=	228.60 cm	=	2.29 m
2 5/8 yards	=	240.03 cm	=	2.40 m
2 3/4 yards	=	251.46 cm	=	2.51 m
2 7/8 yards	=	262.88 cm	=	2.63 m
3 yards	=	274.32 cm	=	2.74 m
3 1/8 yards	=	285.75 cm	=	2.86 m
3 1/4 yards	=	297.18 cm	=	2.97 m
3 3/8 yards	=	308.61 cm	=	3.09 m
3 1/2 yards	=	320.04 cm	=	3.20 m
3 5/8 yards	=	331.47 cm	=	3.31 m
3 3/4 yards	=	342.90 cm	=	3.43 m
3 7/8 yards	=	354.32 cm	=	3.54 m
4 yards	=	365.76 cm	=	3.66 m
4 1/8 yards	=	377.19 cm	=	3.77 m
4 1/4 yards	=	388.62 cm	=	3.89 m
4 3/8 yards	=	400.05 cm	=	4.00 m
4 1/2 yards	=	411.48 cm	=	4.11 m
4 5/8 yards	=	422.91 cm	=	4.23 m
4 3/4 yards	=	434.34 cm	=	4.34 m
4 7/8 yards	=	445.76 cm	=	4.46 m
5 yards	=	457.20 cm	=	4.57 m

E-mail: Customer_Service@whitebirches.com

A Rainbow of Quilts is published by House of White Birches, 306 East Parr Road, Berne, IN 46711, telephone (260) 589-4000. Printed in USA. Copyright © 2004 House of White Birches.

HOUSE of WHITE BIRCHES PUBLISHERS SINCE 1947

RETAILERS: If you would like to carry this pattern book or any other House of White Birches publications, call the Wholesale Department at Annie's Attic to set up a direct account: (903) 636-4303. Also, request a complete listing of publications available from House of White Birches.

Every effort has been made to ensure that the instructions in this pattern book are complete and accurate. We cannot, however, take responsibility for human error, typographical mistakes or variations in individual work.

ISBN: 1-59217-043-9

2 3 4 5 6 7 8 9

STAFF

Editors: Jeanne Stauffer, Sandra L. Hatch
Associate Editor: Dianne Schmidt
Technical Artist: Connie Rand
Copy Editors: Michelle Beck, Nicki Lehman, Conor Allen
Graphic Arts Supervisor: Ronda Bechinski

Graphic Artist: Debby Keel
Art Director: Brad Snow
Assistant Art Director: Karen Allen
Photography: Tammy Christian, Kelly Wiard, Christena Green
Photo Stylist: Tammy Nussbaum